SPRING!

SEASONS OF THE YEAR

by
Harriet Brundle

SEASONS OF THE YEAR

©2016
Book Life
King's Lynn
Norfolk
PE30 4LS

ISBN: 978-1-910512-54-8

Printed in China

Written by:
Harriet Brundle

Edited by:
Gemma McMullen

Designed by:
Drue Rintoul

A catalogue record for this book is available from the British Library.

Contents

Page Title

4   Seasons of the Year
6   Spring
8   The Weather
10 Plants
12 Animals
14 In the Garden
16 Food
18 What do we Wear in Spring?
20 Things to do in Spring
22 Fun in Spring
24 Glossary & Index

Words that appear like **this** can be *found* in the glossary on page 24.

Seasons of the Year

There are four seasons in a year. The seasons are called Spring, Summer, Autumn and Winter.

Each season is different. This book will tell you about Spring!

5

Spring

Spring happens after Winter and before Summer. The months of Spring are March, April and May.

spring

January

Sun	Mon	Tue	Wed	Thu	Fri	Sat
1	2	3	4	5	6	7
8	9	10	11	12	13	14
15	16	17	18	19	20	21
22	23	24	25	26	27	28
29	30	31				

February

Sun	Mon	Tue	Wed	Thu	Fri	Sat
			1	2	3	4
5	6	7	8	9	10	11
12	13	14	15	16	17	18
19	20	21	22	23	24	25
26	27	28	29			

March

Sun	Mon	Tue	Wed	Thu	Fri	Sat
			1	2	3	
4	5	6	7	8	9	10
11	12	13	14	15	16	17
18	19	20	21	22	23	24
25	26	27	28	29	30	31

April

Sun	Mon	Tue	Wed	Thu	Fri	Sat
	2	3	4	5	6	7
	9	10	11	12	13	14
16	17	18	19	20	21	
23	24	25	26	27	28	
	30					

May

Sun	Mon	Tue	Wed	Thu	Fri	Sat
		1	2	3	4	5
6	7	8	9	10	11	12
13	14	15	16	17	18	19
20	21	22	23	24	25	26
27	28	29	30	31		

June

Sun	Mon	Tue	Wed	Thu	Fri	Sat
					1	2
3	4	5	6	7	8	9
10	11	12	13	14	15	16
17	18	19	20	21	22	23
24	25	26	27	28	29	30

July

Sun	Mon	Tue	Wed	Thu	Fri	Sat
	2	3	4	5	6	7
	9	10	11	12	13	14
16	17	18	19	20	21	
23	24	25	26	27	28	
29	30	31				

August

Sun	Mon	Tue	Wed	Thu	Fri	Sat
		1	2	3	4	
6	7	8	9	10	11	
12	13	14	15	16	17	18
20	21	22	23	24	25	
	27	28	29	30	31	

September

Sun	Mon	Tue	Wed	Thu	Fri	Sat
						1
2	3	4	5	6	7	8
9	10	11	12	13	14	15
16	17	18	19	20	21	22
23	24	25	26	27	28	29
30						

October

Sun	Mon	Tue	Wed	Thu	Fri	Sat
1	2	3	4	5	6	
8	9	10	11	12	13	
15	16	17	18	19	20	
22	23	24	25	26	27	
29	30	31				

November

Sun	Mon	Tue	Wed	Thu	Fri	Sat
			1	2	3	
5	6	7	8	9	10	
12	13	14	15	16	17	
19	20	21	22	23	24	
26	27	28	29	30		

December

Sun	Mon	Tue	Wed	Thu	Fri	Sat
						1
3	4	5	6	7	8	
10	11	12	13	14	15	
17	18	19	20	21	22	
24	25	26	27	28	29	
31						

Each day in Spring has more hours of sunlight than the last. This makes the daytime feel longer.

The Weather

The weather starts to get warmer in Spring.

There is rain in Springtime. If the sun is also shining, it makes a rainbow!

Plants

As the weather starts to get warmer in Spring, the flowers and plants grow.

The rain in Springtime gives the plants water so they can grow bigger.

Animals

Some animals have their babies in Spring.

Which of these animal babies have you seen before?

Lamb

Chick

Calf

Animals must eat plenty to make milk for their babies.

Udder

In the Garden

When the sun is shining,
we can play in the garden.

In Spring, we can plant seeds in the garden to grow different fruits, vegetables and plants.

Food

Lots of different fruits and vegetables are ready to be eaten in Spring.

Fruits and vegetables are good for us.

Rhubarb

Apples

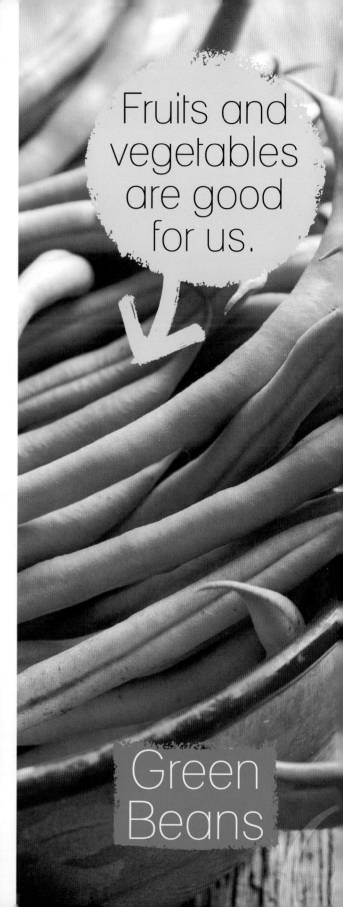

Green Beans

Spring greens are a type of cabbage that are perfect for eating in Spring.

What do we Wear in Spring?

Even if the sun is shining, Spring can be chilly! We might need a jumper.

Jumper

Umbrella

Rain Coat

Don't forget your coat and umbrella if it is raining!

Things to do in Spring

Christians celebrate Easter in Spring. It is exciting to have an egg hunt!

It is fun to go to the farm in Spring. You might get to see an animal being born.

21

Fun in Spring

Draw pictures of the different types of weather you might see in Spring. What might you be wearing in each picture?

Look out for these Spring flowers in the garden or the park!

Fun Fact

In Spring, the birds sing more than at any other time!

Dandelion

Daffodil

23

Glossary

Plenty: lots of something.

Rainbow: a curved shape of different colours seen in the sky when the sun is shining and it is also raining.

Udder: the part of a cow where a calf gets milk from.

Index

Rain 9, 11, 19

Season 4, 5

Sun 9, 14, 18

Weather 8, 10, 22

Photo credits

Photocredits: Abbreviations: l-left, r-right, b-bottom, t-top, c-centre, m-middle. All images are courtesy of Shutterstock.com.
Front Cover, 5 – Sunny studio. 1 - Sunny studio. 2 - Elenamiv. 3 - Poznyakov. 4l Konstanttin. 4lc – djgis. 4rc – Smileus. 4r – Triff. 6 – JonesHon. 7 – ilikestudio. 8 – Mira Arnaudova. 9 – Preto Perola. 10 – djgis. 10bl – Erik Lam. 10bc – yevgeniy11. 10br - Eric Isselee. 11 - Dudarev Mikhail. 11inset - viktori-art. 12 – chikapylka. 12inset - Maya Kruchankova. 13 – LiliGraphie. 14 – Rawpixel.15 – racorn. 15inset - Ilizia. 16l – Mark Bridger. 16c - Tomo Jesenicnik. 16r - Jiri Hera. 17 – Chamille White. 17inset - pedalist. 18 – Maria Evseyeva. 19 – FamVeld. 20 – Kzenon. 21 – SunKids. 22b - Anan Kaewkhammul. 22r - Denphumi. 23t - Eric Isselee. 23l - Quang Ho. 23r - Jessmine.